# My Favourite

Written by Lisa Thompson
Pictures by Luke Jurevicius and Arthur Moody

My favourite colour is red.

I like the red leaves.

3

I like green best.

My hair is green.

5

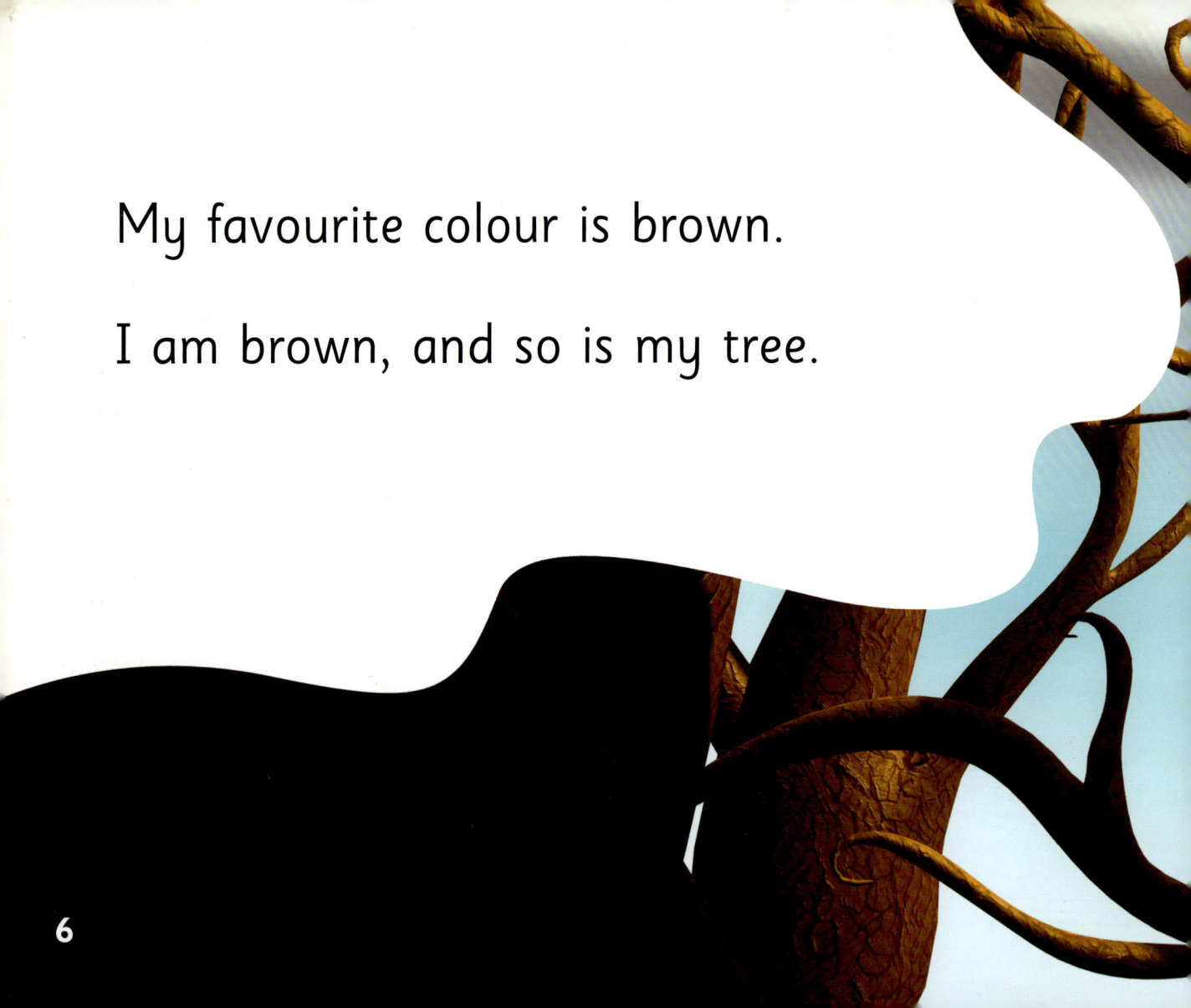

My favourite colour is brown.

I am brown, and so is my tree.

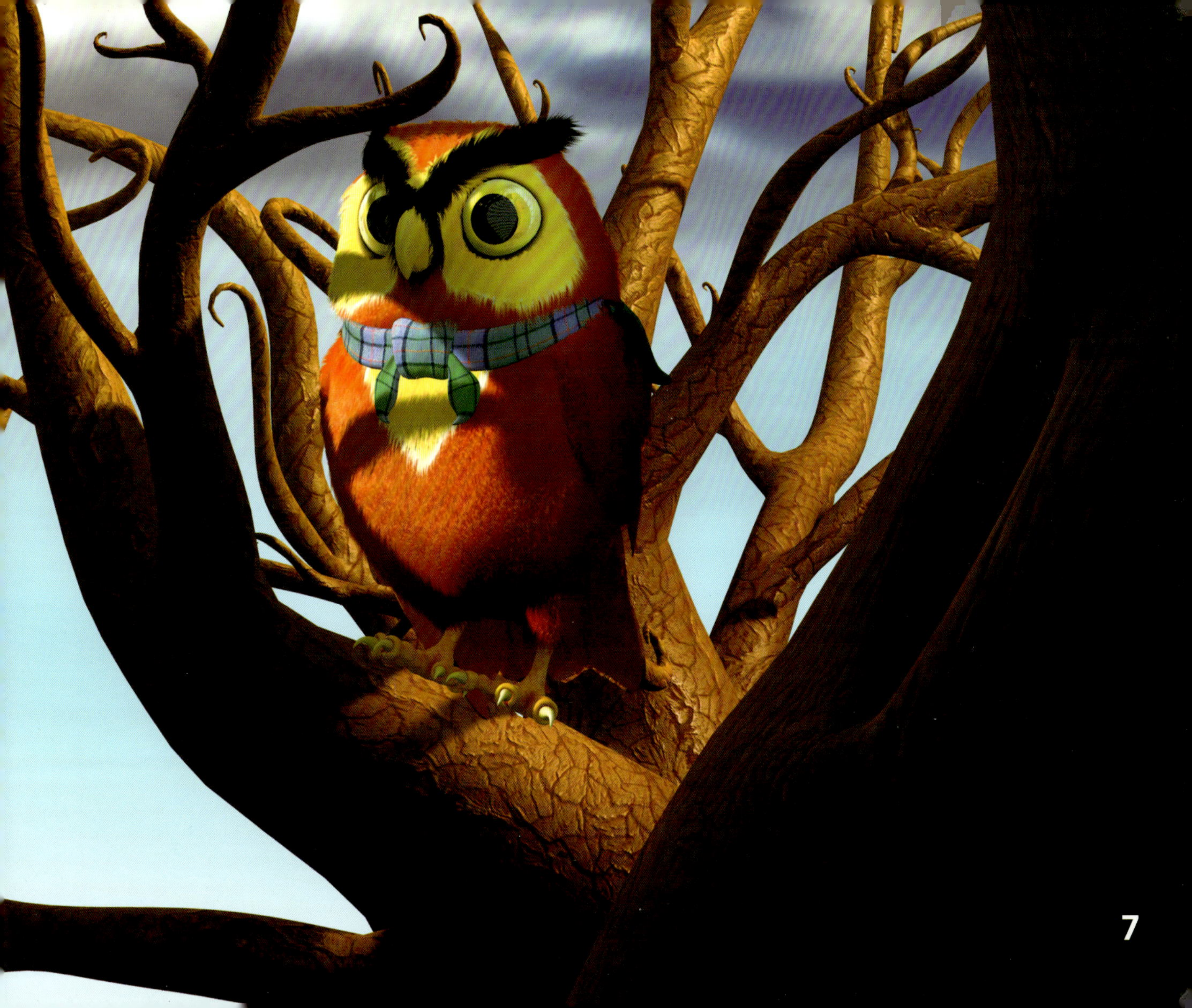

My beak is yellow,
and my legs are yellow.

I like the yellow in the sky, too.

9

My favourite colour is yellow, too.

Look at the big yellow moon.

11

I like it here, under my bridge.

There are **dark** colours here.

13

Look at all the colours in the rainbow.

I like **all** the colours!

15

**Match Me!**

I like green.

I like red.

I like brown.

16